Forest Fires

by Janet Piehl

PULL AHEAD BOOKS
Forces of Nature

Lerner Publications Company • Minneapolis

For Cathy Starr

Photo Acknowledgments

The images in this book are used with the permission of: © Karl Weatherly/PhotoDisc/Getty Images, pp. 1, all backgrounds; © Robert Sciarrino/Star Ledger/CORBIS, p. 4; © Raymond Gehman/CORBIS, pp. 6, 18; © Karlene Schwartz, pp. 7, 11, 27; National Park Service Photo by Jeff Henry, pp. 8, 12; AP Photo/Dr. Scott M. Lieberman, p. 9; © W. Cody/CORBIS, p. 10; AP Photo/Yakima Herald-Republic, Andy Sawyer, p. 14; © Michael Darter/Photonica/Getty Images, p. 15; © Pedro Armestre/AFP/Getty Images, p. 16; © Dave Waters/ZUMA Press, p. 19; © George Frey/AFP/Getty Images, p. 20; National Park Service Photo by Jim Peaco, p. 21; U.S. Fish & Wildlife Service, p. 22; © Drew Kelly/Stone/Getty Images, p. 24; © Lawrence Migdale/Photo Researchers, Inc., p. 26.

Front Cover: © Michael Quinton/Minden Pictures/Getty Images.
Back Cover: © Karl Weatherly/PhotoDisc/Getty Images
Copyright © 2008 Lerner Publishing Group, Inc.

Lerner Publications Company
A division of Lerner Publishing Group, Inc.
241 First Avenue North
Minneapolis, MN 55401 U.S.A.

Website address: www.lernerbooks.com

Words in **bold type** are explained in a glossary on page 31.

Library of Congress Cataloging-in-Publication Data

Piehl, Janet.
    Forest fires / by Janet Piehl.
        p.   cm. – (Pull ahead books. Forces of nature)
    Includes index.
    ISBN-13: 978−0−8225−7907−6 (lib. bdg. : alk. paper)
    1. Forest fires—Juvenile literature. I. Title.
  SD421.23.P524 2008
  634.9'618−dc22   2007024903

Manufactured in the United States of America
1 2 3 4 5 6 − JR − 13 12 11 10 09 08

Table of Contents

What Is a Forest Fire?

It is a hot, windy day in the forest. It has not rained in weeks. A **spotter** watches from a tall lookout tower. He can see far into the distance. The spotter sees smoke. Part of the forest is burning. How did the forest fire start?

A fire needs **oxygen**, **fuel**, and heat to start. Oxygen is a gas in the air. Fuel is anything that will burn.

Trees and other plants are fuel in the forest.

A fire starts when fuel and oxygen get very hot.

Zap! Lightning strikes a tree. The lightning heats the fuel. A fire starts in the forest.

People cause most forest fires. Someone may toss a burning cigarette into the forest. Heat from the cigarette sets fuel on fire.

Or campers might not put out their campfire completely. Heat from the campfire sets fuel on fire.

The Fire Grows

The wind blows. It carries **sparks** to other parts of the forest. The fire spreads. The fire will burn and grow as long as it has fuel and oxygen. Flames destroy grasses, leaves, and trees.

Many animals live in forests. The fire
burns the animals' homes. Some animals
hide underground. Others run away.

People live in forests too. A fire may burn the people's houses. People must leave the forest.

Firefighters remove fuel to keep a
fire from spreading.

Putting Out Forest Fires

Firefighters put out forest fires. First, they must keep the fire from spreading. They make a **firebreak**. They clear a path in the forest. They remove fuel down to the ground. There is nothing left for the fire to burn. The fire cannot cross the firebreak.

Firefighters spray water or special chemicals on the flames. Water and chemicals remove heat and oxygen. Then the fire can no longer burn.

Sometimes airplanes or helicopters drop water or chemicals on the forest fire.

Rain can help firefighters put out a fire. The rainwater takes heat and oxygen away from the fire.

The fire is finally out. Soon new plants sprout. Animals begin to return to the forest.

Fire Season

Most forest fires burn during **fire season**. Fire season can last from early spring until late fall. During fire season, the weather is often hot and dry. Dry fuel burns easily.

Preventing Forest Fires

You can help to prevent forest fires.
Do not play with matches when you are
in the forest. Make sure your campfire
is completely cool before you leave.

Always tell a parent or a **park ranger** if you see fire in the forest. Then leave the area.

A park ranger

You can help make forests safe places for people, plants, and animals.

More about Forest Fires

A fire needs fuel, oxygen, and heat to start. Scientists call these three things the fire triangle. A triangle has three sides. It will fall apart if one of its sides is taken away. Think about how firefighters put out fires. They remove heat and oxygen by putting water on a fire. They remove fuel by making firebreaks. A fire will go out if one of its parts is removed.

FOREST FIRE FACTS

- Forest fires are dangerous. But they are a natural part of life in the forest. They remove dead trees, leaves, and branches. This makes room for new plants to grow.

- Sometimes forest workers set fires on purpose. These fires destroy the fuel that causes big blazes. Workers watch the fires carefully and put them out safely.

- One of the worst forest fires took place around Peshtigo, Wisconsin, in 1871. About 1,500 people died. Nearly 4.25 million acres of forest burned. That is an area about the size of the state of Delaware.

- A kind of tree called lodgepole pine needs forest fires to start growing. The tree makes cones with seeds inside them. The heat of a forest fire opens the cones and lets out the seeds. The seeds grow into new lodgepole pines.

- Did you know that some forest fires burn underground? This kind of fire is called a ground fire.

Further Reading

Books

Demarest, Chris L. *Hotshots!* New York: Margaret K. McElderry Books, 2003.

Erlbach, Arlene. *Forest Fires*. Danbury, CT: Children's Press, 1995.

Rivera, Sheila. *Forest*. Minneapolis: Lerner Publications Company, 2005.

Websites

National Geographic for Kids–Wildfires
http://magma.nationalgeographic.com/ngexplorer/0111/adventures
This forest fire website includes photos, videos, and audio clips.

Only You Can Prevent Wildfires: Smokey Kids
http://www.smokeybear.com/kids
Learn about forests and Smokey Bear, then play forest fire games.

Wildfires: Prescribed Burns
http://www.fema.gov/kids/wildfire.htm
Learn more about forest fires and how to keep them from happening.

Glossary

firebreak: a path that is cleared in order to stop a fire. Trees and other things that can burn are taken out of this path.

fire season: the time of year when most forest fires happen. It is usually a time of year when it does not rain much. It can be from early spring to late fall.

fuel: anything that can burn

oxygen: a gas in the air we breathe

park ranger: a person whose work is looking after a forest or a park

sparks: small bits of burning matter thrown off by a fire

spotter: a worker whose job is to watch for forest fires. He or she may watch from a high tower or from an airplane.

Index